BLUE WATER OPS

BLUE WATER OPS

ON THE FRONT LINE OF U.S. NAVAL AVIATION

Erik Hildebrandt

Howell Press

BLUE WATER OPS is dedicated to my father Robert Hildebrandt for giving me the ambition to become whatever I want.

Designed by Anthony Brandenburg, Ravenwood Studios.
Edited by Ross A. Howell, Jr. and Jamie L. Bronner.

Library of Congress Catalog Card Number: 97-743554

ISBN 1-57427-061-3

Printed in Hong Kong.
Published by Howell Press, Inc., 1147 River Road, Suite 2, Charlottesville, VA 22901,
telephone (804) 977-4006.

First Printing

Acknowledgments

I first must thank my parents, Judy and Bob, who instilled in me the resolve necessary to find any level of success as a freelance artist. By their examples, I learned how to recognize opportunity and how best to develop those chances once exposed. During the frequent dry spells between creative clarity, my folks afforded me a touchstone of familiarity from which all of my bids for success have been launched. It is a testament to their competence as a parental team that this book was ever made at all. It makes me proudest of all to be able to present them with this achievement.

Special thanks to:

George Hall, who was instrumental in lighting the NAVAIR fire within me. Over the years, his wonderful images twisted the screws of envy and fueled my ambition to crack the code.

Ross and Elinor Howell, my publishers, for not publishing any of the many carrier books they have been pitched over the past twelve years.

Gary Gold, for the priceless education on how to survive in this business while maintaining a sense of humor, if not sanity.

Jim Harker, for helping to hook me up with my first carrier ride.

My friends at CHINFO: CDR Steve Pietropaoli for having the faith in my work to support my endless requests. LCDR Rob Newell, for going to bat for me over and over. Lt. Dave McCulloch and Lt. Erick Goss, for all the legwork that was required in affording me such great access.

The Third Fleet PAO staff, CDR Paul Weishaupt, Lt. Jeff Bender, and Lt. Lisa Brackenbury, for coordinating my many visits with the East Coast fleet.

AIRLANT and CDR Kevin Wensing, for providing me with the chance to experience the flight of a lifetime.

The guys at VA-75, the Sunday Punchers, and specifically Lt. Pat Day and LCDR Tom Dacey, for the cat and the trap that initiated me as a Navy tailhooker.

PACFLEET, specifically CDR Keith Arterburn and LCDR Rich Marin, for working their own PAO magic during RIMPAC '96.

All the hundreds of officers and enlisted people I have met along the way who helped me see their own personal universe while underway.

Richard Wazkiewicz and Kerry Leppo at Randolph Engineering, and Leo Unruh at GENTEX for their generous support in making this book.

But besides all these fine folks who made the book possible, I must reserve my most sincere thanks for my wife, Christine. Her tremendous capacity for understanding the intricacies of this project and the lavish support she has afforded me redefines the word commitment. Thank you does not begin to convey my appreciation.

Preface

This past year I was invited into a world where going to work means putting your life on the line day and night. Adrenaline spikes your senses, widens your eyes into golf balls, and stands your hair on end as you maneuver between volcanic jet blast and menacing prop blades. The carrier flight deck is unlike any workplace in the world. It is exhausting duty that leaves you exhilarated, yet spent; scared to death, yet ecstatic.

Standing in the waist catwalk by catapults 3 and 4, you watch Tomcats and Intruders strain against the holdback bar, engines turning at full power. In an instant, a small plug of steel snaps and a fifty thousand-pound fire breather lurches forward, triggering a reflex that forces you to your knees just in time to see the shadow of the wing passing over you. As the burner blast tries to scoop you up, a grin takes hold of your face. You look around at the eighteen- and nineteen-year-old enlisted "kids" working the catapult gear and you notice they all have the same smile. "Catface," they call it.

This book marks the end of my carrier embarks for a while. I grew very fond of my visits to the fleet and I already miss the many friends I made. By publishing this book I get to share my experiences with all of you. While that's exciting, I am reluctant to wrap up production and turn in my ticket to the boat.

It's no mystery why I make pictures. They enable me to immerse myself in unique situations and string together an endless chain of once-in-a-lifetime experiences. Making the photographs for BLUE WATER OPS, however, will remain at the top of my list for some time to come.

This book is not intended as a comprehensive look at carrier life. It simply offers a glimpse into the world that I was able to access through the lenses of my cameras. I have attempted to include captions and text that offer insight into the mystery of the flight deck. I also have enlisted the help of some of my new friends. They are the pilots and crews who took the time to write essays about their carrier experiences.

For those aspects of carrier operations that are not presented here, I regret not having a thousand pages to fill with the grind and glory of life below the "03." I know it will be said by some of the enlisted men

LCDR Tom Dacey took this picture of me as proof of my qualification as a "tailhooker." Thanks, "Space."

and women as well as the chiefs that this is just another "air-dale" rag. I know all you guys, men and women, are down there greasing the machine. Some of you are playing chess with the planes in the hangar bays; others are logging the pendant hits on the arresting gear. There are countless essential duties that keep these cities at sea underway and to omit one is to omit a thousand.

The images that appear here represent about one percent of the total pictures I shot over the span of this project. I pushed the shutter release on my cameras around fourteen thousand times, which translates into about four hundred rolls of film. While the physical challenges I faced shooting this book were significant, the most challenging part of the project for me was editing the pictures. It has taken me almost as much time and energy to cut the book down to these final frames as it did to expose the film.

Having said all that, it is my sincere pleasure to present BLUE WATER OPS.

—Erik Hildebrandt

My first embark aboard the USS CARL VINSON (CVN-70) en route to Hawaii.

Foreword

This stunning book celebrates the marriage of the airplane and the steam warship. This marriage was a natural. From its infancy, the airplane seemed to offer a way to answer the centuries-old question, What lies over the horizon?

The first aerial pioneer who managed to successfully land a heavier-than-air craft aboard a ship and take it off again was stunt pilot Eugene Ely, who did the deed in 1911 on a U.S. Navy cruiser anchored in San Francisco Bay. It was a portent of things to come.

Soon aircraft were being launched from wooden platforms built atop gun turrets: they crash-landed in the ocean upon their return. This use of the airplane for one-time scouting expeditions was expensive, dangerous, and rarely productive.

Seeking to provide eyes for its battleship fleet, in 1913 Britain converted an elderly light cruiser, HMS *Hermes*, to operate aircraft equipped with floats. The United States didn't acquire its first carrier until 1922, when it converted a collier, *Jupiter*, to operate aircraft with conventional landing gear. The ship was renamed *Langley* in honor of the former head of the Smithsonian Institution, Samuel Langley, who claimed he had flown prior to the Wright brothers. (He didn't, but that's another story.)

Carriers came of age in World War II, when they replaced battleships as the centerpieces around which fleets were built. As aviation progressed from biplane fighters to supersonic jets, the value of the carrier steadily increased. Today carriers take airpower to wherever on the globe it is needed. Even as you read this, somewhere on the oceans of the earth a carrier is launching and recovering aircraft as a routine military operation.

The word "routine" is misleading. Despite the fact that airplanes have been flying from carrier decks since 1913, despite the fact that the ships have grown into specialized leviathans, despite the fact that the aircraft are supersonic jets capable of delivering nuclear weapons or launching guided missiles at stupendous ranges, carrier operations are routine only in the sense that they happen frequently. Launching a fixed-wing aircraft from a ship moving in a seaway and landing it back aboard, fair weather or foul, day or

Intruder in the groove. LCDR Tom Dacey calls the ball on the USS ENTERPRISE.

night, are tasks that are generally acknowledged to be the most challenging in aviation. That anyone other than highly skilled test pilots can do it is a tribute to the training the Navy gives its aviators.

Until you board an aircraft carrier you cannot truly comprehend the reality of this steel city that moves freely on the world's oceans, through wind and storm, through darkness and sunlight, moves wherever the elected officials who guide our nation direct. Nothing ashore prepares you for the sounds, smells, and sights of the ship. They assault your senses, overwhelm you, stun you into awed silence.

As many as 6,000 men and women live and work on a modern carrier, somehow finding space for themselves amid the ninety-plus planes, thousands of tons of jet fuel, bombs, bullets, missiles, spare parts, tools, computers, food, soft drinks, movies, books; almost every item produced by our high-tech civilization is aboard in quantities large or small, tucked in, crammed in somehow, so the pilots, mechanics, quartermasters, engineers, boilermakers, clerks, doctors, dentists, machinists, radar repairmen, clergymen, cooks, bosun's mates, parachute riggers, and all the rest can keep the people fed, healthy, and working and the planes flying.

So you walk through the narrow passageways, taking it in, inhaling it, listening to the strange noises, trying to understand. Finally your guide leads you onto an observation platform on the ship's island. There before you is the large, crowded flight deck with its hundreds of people tending the snorting, fire-belching airplanes that are the reason this ship exists.

Dozens of jet engines at idle, or being goosed up for taxi power, create an unearthly wail. Without ear protection a person would soon go deaf. Amid the planes is a veritable army of people, all busy doing incomprehensible, essential tasks that are necessary to get these planes ready to fly.

The airplanes taxi slowly toward the catapults. Once on a catapult, each pilot winds up his engines to full cry as focused, white-hot flames erupt from the exhausts. The engines sing thunderous songs of almost infinite power. Even through the sound suppressors the noise is extraordinarily loud, a soul-numbing crescendo that vibrates your skin, your flesh, your bones. Then the plane screams down the cat into the waiting sky, and another comes forward for its turn.

Airborne at last, the airplanes climb away, the engine songs fade, and finally they are gone, out of sound and sight somewhere over the sea. On the flight deck you are left with the whisper of the wind, the cry of gulls, and the sound of human voices, somehow so puny, yet oh, so welcome.

Now comes the waiting.

On the flight deck, in the heart of the ship in air traffic control, in the combat information center, on the bridge, in machinery and working spaces throughout the ship, everyone waits. For some of the ship's personnel this interlude is a time of rest, for others a time to catch up on personal correspondence or official paperwork. For some, however, it is a time to think of those aloft.

Those people aloft are in a unique, lonely world. Strapped to an ejection seat in a cramped cockpit of a warplane over an eternal sea on a dismal, miserable night when the sky is cloud from sea to stratosphere, when the rain comes in sheets, when the wind gusts and the restless sea makes even the largest ship roll and heave, here a person is truly, absolutely alone, with no one to rely upon but himself. Here the word night takes on a whole new meaning: there is not a speck of light out there, nothing. Not a glimmer, not a single tiny glow, not even a faint, distant star. The night is as black and lonely as the grave.

Yes, the people on the ship are down there somewhere to talk to via radio, and there are other pilots aloft in this infinite night, but here, in the cockpit, the pilot has only his skill, his courage, his ability to think and to cope and to fly this airplane. His very survival depends on these assets.

At night, above a hungry sea, a pilot thinks of these things. And of home, and loved ones waiting, somewhere, back in the real world.

Is there an occupation anywhere more unforgiving of human error? One wonders.

Finally the planes return to the ship.

Standing on the flight deck on a brisk day at sea, you first hear the engines moaning above the sound of the wind, then you see them, specks against the clouds and blue. They stream in closer and closer, queuing up.

The first one turns onto the glide slope above the ship's wake, its landing gear and hook down, flaps and slats hanging from the wings, speed brakes out, the engine's song subtly rising and falling as the pilot works the throttle to stay on the glide slope. And then it is here, crossing the ramp with its main wheels feeling for the deck, the hook reaching for an arresting gear wire.

The hook catches! As the pilot jams the throttle to full power--just in case--the hook drags the plane to a quivering halt.

Back! Down and safe!

The pilots will tell you that flying around the ship is routine--there's that word again. It's safe, they say. Done properly, by skilled people who are part of a highly trained team, it is indeed routine. But when a ship sails out of range of divert fields ashore, the safety net is gone. In mid-ocean there is no dry place on earth the planes can reach when their fuel is down to landing weight. They must successfully trap aboard their ship . . . or else.

The flight crews have a name for this type of operation: "blue water ops." On the trapeze without a safety net, there is no such thing as "good enough." Second best will not hack the program. You can do it or you can't--there is no in between. This is the challenge of naval aviation, the attraction that draws the best people in the military and holds them through long cruises, through long family separations.

The next best thing to being there and seeing it with your own eyes, hearing it with your own ears, are the photographs of Erik Hildebrandt, a superbly talented young photographer who took his camera when he went to sea.

His photographs amaze me. I have seen the ships and planes so many times, so many ways, yet his photographs make it once again fresh and new. The experience becomes so real I could almost feel the hot blast of jet exhaust, smell it, taste it. Hildebrandt takes me back to the ship, out on the wide sea.

He'll take you there too, in the pages of this book, a paean to the glorious adventure that is carrier aviation.

—Stephen Coonts

A Hornet from VFA-94 aboard the USS KITTY HAWK breaks right over the Pacific during RIMPAC '96 air ops.

Getting the Quals

In order to fly over water in U.S. Navy aircraft, all personnel must complete a rigorous lecture and practical training program. After being examined by a navy flight surgeon and granted an "up chit," candidates are scheduled into a class at the nearest Aviation Physiology and Water Survival School. Since I was to fly with an east coast squadron, my training was scheduled at NAS Norfolk.

I had heard one horror story after another about the class and seen films like *An Officer and a Gentleman*, where trainees seemed to be routinely brought to the brink of drowning. Determined not to be excluded from my opportunity to fly, I spent the two weeks before my class running and working out.

Fifteen of us showed up on the first morning of our first day. We signed in and were escorted to the main classroom of a modern and well designed building. After the obligatory "welcome aboard" orientation speech, the lectures began. We received a barrage of lessons on G-LOC, oxygen deprivation, night vision, emergency equipment uses, etc. I had envisioned those old, boring military training films that had the effect of tranquilizers. But I'm happy to report that the curriculum was delivered by engaging young professionals who were clearly knowledgeable, both in the material as well as in current teaching methods.

Lessons were divided up by frequent stretching breaks, which kept everyone alert. By midmorning we were ready for our first device. One lecture had discussed the effects of oxygen deprivation during unpressurized flight at altitude. To enable us to recognize the symptoms, we made a simulated flight to 25,000 feet in the hypobaric chamber. During "ascent," we breathed pure oxygen through standard-issue flight crew masks and regulators. Once we were at altitude, the masks were removed and we were instructed to play patty-cake with the person beside us.

Within four minutes, the body's inability to absorb adequate oxygen from the reduced air pressure causes a variety of reactions. Some people's lips turned blue, as did their fingernails. My partner suddenly stopped playing patty-cake and stared at the wall on the opposite side of the chamber. His hands were still stretched out and both were twitching involuntarily, just what our instructors had predicted might happen. When muscles are starved for oxygen, they begin to act independently of the mind in regular, sudden pulses.

I found myself unable to concentrate. Hot flashes caused me to break out in a cold sweat. My arms felt very tired and it became difficult to hold them up. After about five minutes, I pulled my oxygen mask back on before experiencing any of the more severe effects of oxygen starvation. People can become giddy or belligerent when the support staff attempt to replace masks. Nobody in our group really freaked out, but I certainly felt the onset of a very serious condition.

The next devices related to emergency egress systems. All of us were outfitted with a flight suit, boots, torso harness, g-suit, helmet, and gloves. The class was broken up into four groups and we were taken to different device stations. My group was first instructed on how to use the ejection seat simulator rail. This device is an operational Martin Baker ejection seat, except that the pyrotechnic gun has been replaced with a compressed nitrogen gas ram. Suited up in full tactical jet flight gear, you are instructed on how to hook up the leg restraints, Koch fittings on the harness, and oxygen/communications cord. After a quick briefing, you are lowered into the mock cockpit. With all items secured and a thumbs up from the operators, the words, "EJECT! EJECT! EJECT!" come over the helmet ICS.

One quick pull of the lower or upper ejection handles sends you blasting up the rail in one hard shot in the pants. It's estimated that the simulator exerts about one-fifth of the g-forces of an actual ejection. Nonetheless, what

Exhausted from all the swimming, this candidate rests after orally inflating his LPU.

I experienced was enough to wrench my spine and daze me just a bit. Then I was lowered to the starting point. The operator calls out, "Emergency EGRESS! Get out! Get out!" and clicks a stopwatch. To qualify, you have ten seconds to release all points of contact with the seat, unhook the leg restraints, g-suit, and helmet cord. Ten seconds pass very quickly, but I was able to complete the tasks in time.

Shuffling down the hall in our flight gear, we were led into the parachute room, where four chute hookups hung from rigs on the ceiling. We snapped the seat pan from an ejection seat onto the lower Koch fittings of the torso harness and climbed up a set of stairs to the parachute hookups. After connecting the upper Kochs to the rigs, we were told to lean into the harness and allow ourselves to hang free of the platforms. Following instructions, we practiced techniques for unfouling the lines of a tangled parachute and steering using the risers. Finally, we unhooked the harnesses and climbed up to a five-foot platform, where we jumped one by one onto a wrestling mat to learn proper landing techniques.

Demonstrations of various night vision phenomena came next. In a darkroom equipped with a specialized slide projector, we were taught how to avoid night blindness and how to adapt for optimum night vision. A series of slides demonstrated the human eye's inability to differentiate colors in low light as well as the benefits of pattern scanning of the horizon.

The final lecture of the day was delivered in conjunction with a demonstration of the survival gear found in the life vests, rafts, and seat packs of Naval aircraft. Radios, mirrors, flares, and food were just a few of the briefs we were given on surviving a crash and aiding in our own rescue. With one last video presentation on underwater egress techniques, we were excused for the day and told to show up first thing in the morning at the pool for water-survival practice and testing out.

By 7:30 A.M. we were in the pool, learning the required strokes and drownproofing techniques. As the instructors became comfortable with our abilities, we were allowed to gear up with flight suits and boots. Again we practiced and again we were told to add equipment: torso harness, g-suit, helmet, survival vest, and gloves. Getting back in the pool with a full complement of gear was like being tossed into a tub of Jell-O. The water seemed to push against your arms and legs as you struggled to keep your mouth above water. Since I grew up on the ocean and am a good swimmer, my comfort in the water made this part of the training less difficult. But a number of my classmates were not at all comfortable with barely being able to stay near the surface.

Most of my classmates felt it was necessary to keep their heads out of the water and quickly tired themselves out trying to do so. The successful technique is to relax and use your own air capacity as flotation, which means that you only raise your head to take a breath. The rest of the time you lie still just beneath

The notorious Helo Dunker has earned the nasty reputation as "Panic in a Can."

the surface. As these tiring swimmers gasped for air, a few sucked in water and began to cough. If the instructors were not confident about your ability to stay afloat, you were gone.

Testing out consisted of swimming just two laps, using any of three approved strokes, followed by two minutes of treading water, and finishing with two minutes of dead man's float. At the end of the float, or "drownproofing," you had to manually inflate your life vest by blowing into the oral filler tube. At this point in the testing, only four candidates were left. Almost all failed out during the two-minute phase of floating and filling the vest.

With these elements of water survival completed, it was on to the 9D5 device. Better known as the "helo dunker," the 9D5 is a fiber glass cylinder with eight seats, configured like a typical multi-place aircraft. There are open windows between every two seats and a main cabin door on the forward right side. The drill requires that everyone must egress the simulator under four separate scenarios. The first is to escape via the nearest exit, be it door or window. The second scenario is to exit via the main cabin door—keep in mind, there are eight seats. The third and fourth escape scenarios are the same as the first two, only now you are wearing swimming goggles—painted black.

These escape scenarios sound simple enough, until you take into account the sequencing of the ride. Once you are strapped into your randomly assigned seat, you assume the crash position: head in your lap and hands holding the sides of the seat. With your stomach already full of butterflies, the dunker is released and free falls to the waterline. The "can" slams to a stop and begins to sink. As water rushes in around your ankles and legs, you grab your seat buckle release and the reference point toward which you are going to make your escape.

Just as the water reaches your chin, you take a full breath. Then the simulator does a terrifying thing. The cylinder rotates upside-down, leaving you hanging from what is now the ceiling. With both hands holding onto critical escape mechanisms, you can't hold your nose, which fills up with water because of the inverted attitude. To keep water out, you blow gently, only to realize that your instincts make you want to breathe back in. So begins the wave of panic as each of us realizes too late that the pool horrors we had heard about are real. After completion of the first escape scenario, any sense of fun has disappeared; angst and fear sour the faces of the four of us who are left.

Full flight gear makes swimming a matter of survival and hauling yourself into a life raft virtually impossible.

While you are upside-down, you cannot exit the device until all motion has stopped. It takes about fifteen seconds from when you take your breath until you are legally able to egress. The penalty for an early escape is a rerun for the violator. They don't call the helo dunker "Panic in a Can" for nothing. During my third run, I lost control of my breathing and made an early egress. After successfully finishing the fourth and final run, I had to redo the third event to get the qual.

At one point, one of the other students emerged from the pool with a gash across his nose, bright red blood running down his flight suit. A typical hazard is to be kicked by other escapees wearing the heavy, steel-toed boots we were issued.

Sitting on the pool bleachers with my head in my hands as water poured from my nasal passages, I was patted on the back by our instructor, who handed me the folder holding the almighty stamp of qualified aircrew. From a class of fifteen, only three of us successfully completed all the tasks that day. Still want to fly off a carrier?

FOD Walk-down

Within the harsh environments where military jet aircraft are expected to operate, precautions are taken to minimize stress on the equipment. The flight deck of a carrier is host to a wide variety of activities. Between flight operations, scheduled maintenance and battle damage repairs are carried out wherever planes are chained down. The entire boat is a workshop.

As a result, there is a constant accumulation of FOD, acronym for "Foreign Object Damage," a term describing anything that could be ingested by the hurricane suction of a jet engine. Common items in maintenance work like tools, safety wire, rivets, etc., are prime FOD culprits.

Personnel are free to roam the flight deck when flight ops are not underway. It's common to see as many as a hundred people running laps around the perimeter of the ship in an effort to maintain physical fitness on these cramped living platforms. Equally as damaging to a jet engine as forgotten tools could be stateroom keys lost while jogging or ceramic shards from a broken coffee cup that someone brought up top while watching a sunset.

The most effective way to pick up this stuff is to call all off-duty personnel onto the flight deck to conduct a FOD walk-down. Every channel on the ship's TVs goes black and flashes a request to participate. The FOD walk-down is announced over the public address system, the IMC, by the deck handler in Flight Deck Control. A walk-down is called before each flight event. Walk-downs are usually sponsored by one of the squadrons, who send a representative to the

All available personnel scour the flight deck for FOD. The device on the left is a rolling magnet for snagging metal.

handler to start the walk and to blast a selection of tunes over the deck address system for motivation. There is always rivalry surrounding the musical selections. Comments fly freely between the different squadrons as the entire group conducts this serious but lighthearted task, cleaning the deck from stem to stern.

Ahead of the walk-down line, a deckhand with an air hose connected to a pipe blows out each of the "pad-eyes" recessed into the flight deck. These tie-down points are notorious for hiding the worst FOD as well as filling up with water, which gets blown everywhere by the jet blast during operations. As the crowd wanders aft, the mini-Zamboni-looking deck scrubbers follow, vacuuming up anything left undetected. Because of the sixty to eighty thousand dollar cost of a jet engine overhaul, FOD is regarded as a genuine threat and is dealt with very seriously.

Sunrise marks the start of a new day, as does the gathering for the morning's first FOD walk-down.

Hornet Launch

The F/A-18 Hornet has a unique and surprising element in its launch procedure.

All around the airplane, white shirt plane checkers crawl under the wings, yanking on ordnance hard points to ensure that couplings are secure. In the cockpit, the pilot follows a deck handler's hand signals, crossing the flight deck to the cat shuttle. On a signal from the launch officer, the pilot throttles up to full military power, a setting two-thirds up the throttle arc, marked by a ten-pound indent. Going beyond the indent will light the afterburners.

With hands held in the air for safety, the pilot looks for the red shirt ordnance guys to give a thumbs up after removing all the safe wires from the payload fuses. As the red shirts retreat from under the plane, the pilot shifts his attention to the launch officer, or "shooter," who scans the area around the jet, waiting for the thumbs up from all the deck spotters and plane checkers. While the shooter scans the deck, the pilot cycles the flight controls and looks into the rearview mirrors mounted on the canopy jamb to confirm proper actuation. With that inspection completed, the pilot looks directly at the shooter and snaps a salute to signal "all go." Then the pilot does the unexpected. He takes his right hand off the stick and places it high on the canopy rail.

A deck handler waves a Hornet up to the shuttle through the steam of the previous launch on the USS ENTERPRISE.

When the Hornet was first delivered to the Navy in the early-eighties, pilots flew this fly-by-wire plane off the ship "hands on," as all planes had been launched in the past. However, there was a sharp increase in the occurrence of PIO (pilot induced oscillation), which claimed a number of jets. Subsequent investigations discovered that the stick input from the pilot upon leaving the catapult was conflicting with input from the Hornet's onboard computer, which is programmed to establish the initial AOA (angle of attack) for optimum flight. Conflicting control inputs could result in ever-widening attitude variation, or oscillation, resulting in instability, or in some cases, a total loss of control.

Above the USS CARL VINSON a waved-off Tomcat screams past a Hornet at full power—notice the pilot gripping the canopy jamb.

Since the Hornet's flight computer can establish the desired initial flight configuration by adjusting for variations in environmental conditions and ship movement more quickly and more consistently than a human pilot, Hornet drivers have been restricted to a hands-off launch procedure. To confirm this status to the shooter, a pilot must place his right hand in full view on the canopy rail. Hornet drivers don't even reach for the stick until after the jet leaves the deck and has established a smooth transition to accelerated ascending flight.

View from the "launch bubble" where the bow cats can be fired in bad weather from the USS CARL VINSON.

Quiet times like this are few and far between. As you walk around the flight deck of the USS ENTERPRISE in the glow of the rising sun, it is hard not to be moved by the beauty and grace of the sights around you.

F/A-18 Hornet from VFA-83 Rampagers, pours on the power in a twilight launch off the bow of the USS ENTERPRISE.

If you look closely, you can see the right hand of this USS ENTERPRISE Sunliners pilot holding the "cat grip" on the canopy jamb.

Dawn patrol off the bow of the USS CARL VINSON.

From the backseat of the Hornet, it is not hard to understand why the airplane is such an effective fighter. Visibility is nearly unobstructed, contributing to a pilot's SA or situational awareness; the dominant catch phrase of any safety or mission brief.

Thirsty Hornets return from a practice strike mission off the North Carolina coast and get some gas from a VA-75 Intruder during work-ups for deployment on the USS ENTERPRISE.

Getting a good picture of any eight planes is lucky enough, but to capture an eight-ship CAG flight where each brightly painted bird is the squadron CO's own ride is almost impossible. Almost.

L SO "Paddles"

This LSO (Landing Signal Officer) is watching a squadron mate from VFA-25's Fist of the Fleet bring his F/A-18 Hornet back aboard the USS CARL VINSON. .
He is actually working the throttles with his left hand, unaware of his unconscious reaction.

Teamwork on the LSO platform is critical to determining if the landing area is clear or foul. (Inset) Monitors throughout the ship show the same picture seen by the LSO. It indicates deviations of lineup and glide slope.

This sequence clearly shows the "paddles" following every move a Tomcat pilot makes while coming back aboard the USS CARL VINSON.

33

Viking

A tanker variant of the S-3 Viking takes up station over the Pacific in support of flight operations during RIMPAC '96. (Inset) During Fleet Week in San Francisco, an S-3 was launched inside the Golden Gate off the USS CARL VINSON.

E ject! Eject! Eject!

To be a nugget Naval fighter pilot, fresh from the Replacement Air Group (RAG) aboard an aircraft carrier for his first cruise, is an amazingly exciting experience. Everything is new and bewildering. Flight operations are intense. In the RAG each training mission is dedicated to a specific mission, i.e., ACM (Air Combat Maneuvering), L/L (Low-Level), in-flight refueling, or CQ (Carrier Qualifications). However, as a fleet pilot, you are required to do multi-mission hops each day.

Usually we receive our flight tasking the night prior to a mission, which allows us time to think about the flight and formulate a game plan. The night of February 21, 1994, I was elated to find myself on the schedule to fly supersonic profiles against the carrier for missile-tracking training and proficiency. Along with the ship's crew receiving training, a cable television film crew was to practice filming aircraft at high speeds for later programs. I was scheduled to brief the flight with my XO (Executive Officer) as the Mission Commander/ Section Lead. Jeff "Ratt" Strobel was my scheduled RIO (Radar Intercept Officer).

We got in the books and determined our performance restrictions. The brief, man-up, and launch went smoothly. The plan was for my Section Lead to pass the ship as a single and then Ratt and I would follow three minutes in trail.

As we approached the ship from the stern we leveled off and started a right turn to pass down the port side and cross the bow of the ship. Directly abeam the ship we felt two distinct thumps, as if we had passed through the jet wash of another aircraft. Immediately we heard the aural tone indicating a compressor stall. My instant reaction was to level the wings and start climbing to slow down and get safe

Lt. Rick Lucas, call sign "Comet," does a preflight walk-around on his F-14D Super Tomcat while flying with VF-11's Red Rippers on the USS CARL VINSON.

An SH-60 "Angel" in starboard defense like this one recovered both Lucas and his RIO and returned them to the USS CARL VINSON within minutes of their mishap.

separation from the water. Ratt confirmed that we had a right engine compressor stall.

Through this period—which lasted about three seconds—I felt fairly calm, thinking that we were not in extreme danger. This feeling changed rapidly, however, once the jet exhibited a mind of its own. It initiated a wing dip, which was not commanded by my stick placement. At this point I'm feeling that the jet may be out of control. If you're flying a supersonic fighter, that's a rather terrifying feeling, to say the least.

I go through my emergency procedures and determine that we've lost our right engine. When I inform Ratt, he immediately asks if I've got it, meaning, do I have control of the jet or not?

I reply, "Hold on," thinking I can regain control. After the first wing dip I tried to counter with the stick. Much to my chagrin, the stick was locked in place. I couldn't budge it. Then the jet made a second wing dip in the opposite direction as the first. Still the stick was locked. I scanned the instruments for the second time and saw that we've lost the flight side (starboard) hydraulics. I report this to Ratt. Again he asks if I've got it.

"Hold on," I said. By now we have separated from the water around 4,000 feet and have decelerated to around 350 KIAS. I have the stick in both hands and with all my strength I'm trying to break it free. Then I hear the dreaded words, "It looks like you are on fire."

As that registered in my mind I looked in the rearview mirror and saw flames on the aft section of the aircraft. I turned my head and saw yes, we are on fire, the entire aft section is aflame. That was when I made the decision I thought I would never have to make. I turned forward and keyed the mike to Ratt.

"We're on fire. EJECT, EJECT, EJECT!"

As I pulled the ejection handle, white smoke filled the cockpit for an instant before I closed my eyes or blacked out, one of the two. The feeling of the severe wind blast is unforgettable. I felt as though my arms were going to be ripped right off my body. Then I felt the beautiful shock of the parachute as it opened above me.

I'm elated to be alive. I quickly check to see that in fact all my appendages are intact and useful. Luckily that is the case. I then scanned the sky for Ratt and found him above and behind me. Not knowing if he is alive and well, I tried yelling at him and kicking and waving my arms to get his attention. I finally received an arm wave back. Thank goodness.

As I pointed towards the ship, which I can see clearly only a few miles away, I prepared for water entry. Hitting the water, I released my parachute and boarded my one-man life raft. Since we were so close to the ship, the helos were right on us as we hit the water. Ratt was picked up first, then me, just a few moments later. Once in the helo, we were flown to the carrier and taken down to medical. Ratt ended up with a broken collar bone, a charred hand, and some cuts on his face. I had a slight bruise on the back of my left calf.

—Lt. Rick Lucas, call sign, "Comet"
VF-11 Red Rippers

*A*ll Hands

A fueling crew, or "grapes" as they are called, gather for a team photo after having just completed the last event of a six-month cruise aboard the USS AMERICA.

In the flight deck environment requiring efficiency and speed, no piece of equipment can replace the brute strength of man power, here being used to park a returning F/A-18.

Air Boss CDR Pete Williams, call sign "Caps," orchestrates all the launch, recovery, and airborne action aboard the USS ENTERPRISE as a Hornet gets waved off.

A F-14D Super Tomcat crew from VF-11 suits up in the parachute rigger's gear locker aboard the USS CARL VINSON. This aviator scribbles a radio frequency on the palm of his hand as his partner pulls on a g-suit.

A greenie ground crew from VS-35 checks out their painted tail CAG bird aboard the USS CARL VINSON on the way to Pearl Harbor.

As the USS AMERICA enters her home port at Norfolk, her entire crew turns out to "man the rail."

After rigging the hold back bar on the nose of an S-3, this green shirt sprints clear for the immediate launch on Cat 4.

The deck handler aboard the USS AMERICA looks over the "Ouija board" used to mark the places of each plane on both the flight deck and hangar level.

The launch crew of Cat 1 on the USS ENTERPRISE waits for the next jet to be directed up to the gear.

The waist Cat on the USS ENTERPRISE launches a Tomcat from the new Jolly Rogers during work-ups for their Med Cruise.

The crash crews have some of the best seats in the house during flight ops. Here the bow crew on the USS CARL VINSON waits out a lull in the action.
(Inset) A Tomcat plane captain waits patiently for the flight crew to come "borrow" his ship for another mission.

Brown shirt "line guys" wipe down this Hornet from VFA-113.

Dodging the volcanic jet blast as well as the hurricane intakes are a matter of life and death that deck crews deal with every day.

Red "ordies" catch some rays during a little down time on a Hornet from VFA-25 aboard the USS CARL VINSON.

An arresting gear crew pulls a fresh "pendant" from the box to replace a worn-out number 3 wire. Every one hundred "hits," the trap wires are stripped and changed.

Intruder line mechanics run some maintanance on an A-6E, part of VA-75, the last operational squadron flying the plane.

The waist shooter vacates his post after launching the last plane of the final fly-off on the USS AMERICA.

Cat 3 on the USS ENTERPRISE sends off a Tomcat late in the day for a "pinky" sunset event.

Recovery

Night traps are accented by a shower of sparks and navigation lights.

A Hornet from VFA-25 comes aboard in the late light en route to Pearl Harbor.

This Hornet driver really put the coals to it after catching a "two wire." Afterburners are usually reserved for airborne maneuvers.

Air Strike on the Enterprise

During a ship's work-up training cycle, every facet of the boat's capability is put on trial, sometimes by designated military aggressor units and other times by the battle group's own assets. On this particular day, the task of playing the part of hostile aircraft falls upon a pair of the battle group's deadliest antishipping platforms—Grumman A-6 Intruders.

"Borg I, Red Eye."

"Red Eye, Borg I. Go ahead."

"Advise when on station. Playtime in one-zero miles."

"Copy."

We had already secured our transponders. Why give the carrier's radar operators an easy time? Two hours earlier, down in the ready room, we had planned to drive away from the USS ENTERPRISE to a point 100 miles out. From there, we would try to sneak toward the carrier and drop six Mk-76 twenty-five-pound practice bombs in the ship's wake—our way of saying, "Gotcha!"

Attacking a ship, however, presents some unique and difficult problems. First of all, there are the fighters. Beyond the ship's radar horizon (due to the curvature of the earth) fighters are the main line of defense. Against them, we have no chance. The Intruder is a bomber, remember, so our best defense is to remain unseen. After the

Ready for the cat stroke, LCDR Tom Dacey, call sign "Space," snaps a salute to the launch officer. Notice his throttle hand wrapped around the "cat grip" to make sure the throttles stay at full power under the intense g-load of the cat stroke.

fighters comes the ship itself. It's a floating arsenal, and the ocean offers no terrain to hide behind. We do, however, have a cloaking device.

"RADALT, going to 150."

"Roger," I answer my pilot, Lt. Patrick Day, as I glance over my right shoulder and spot our wingman tucked in tightly. By flying extremely low, we reduce any radar return to an airborne radar emitter (fighter). This makes it extremely difficult to pick us up in the clutter from the particularly choppy sea surface (what luck!).

"Borg 1 and 2 on station," I transmit. "Red Eye copies. PLAY BALL,

PLAY BALL."

Our wingman, Borg 2, splits away and takes up position one mile abeam of us while we quickly turn to a heading not directly toward the carrier, but on a forty-five degree cut in front of her. Since they expect us to go for the wake, the majority of the search will be in that direction.

"Borg 1, Red Eye. Radio check."

"Borg 1, loud and clear." Pat looks over at me, and although an oxygen mask covers most of his face, I can see he is grinning.

"Our own guys can't see us," crackles over the ICS. I grin back.

"Borg 1, Red Eye. Picture: single group, bearing 050 for 40, nose hot."

Enemy fighters. Ahead of us and slightly right; forty miles away and approaching. I respond with a quick succession of two microphone clicks; the universal sign for "Roger." I want to keep voice transmissions to a minimum. The ENTERPRISE has an impressive array of detection devices; including DF (Direction Finding) equipment. The longer I transmit, the easier it will be for them to find our direction of approach, and send fighters our way.

I refigure the carrier's position. "Bring it right 10."

"Right 10," Pat responds and I feel the plane dip slightly.

Borg 2 holds his position through the course change. The radars in both Intruders are off. At this altitude and range, we would never get a radar return, even from something as big as an aircraft carrier. The ship, however, would detect a signal from us with no problem. I have to remember which way the ship is going, calculate how far it can travel based on last observed speed, take the effect of wind on us and the ship, apply those calculations within the time it takes for us to go out and come back, and lead our two-plane assault force to the correct point.

In other words, I guess.

Radar operators down in the ship's CDC probe the skies for telltale blips on their screens.

Our cloaking device: confusion.

"Sixty-five miles," I say in my most confident voice.

"Roger."

After about forty-five seconds, we hear another transmission.

"Borg 1, Red Eye. Picture: single group, 035 for 19, nose hot."

Click, click.

The reason to have a wingman keep position a mile abeam is for efficient lookout. We can easily look directly behind our wingman's aircraft, the most likely approach for an enemy fighter. When we arrive at a point fifteen miles from the ship, Borg 2 will slide into position directly behind us. This way, the radar beam from the ship may only see one attacker.

Blooooop!

The fighters are looking for us in earnest. Their radars are on. (We have radar detectors, too.)

"Twenty-eight miles. Bring it right another 10."

"Right 10. Keep an eye out."

"We're invisible, man!" I respond. "Nothing can get us now."

A minute later, Borg 2 moves behind us and slips from sight. By my calculation, we are 13.5 miles from the carrier. Still no fighters to be seen. Cool. Pat jams the throttles to full power and reefs back on the control stick. The Intruder soars to 1,500 feet as he rolls the plane inverted and pulls to stop our climb. At the top of the maneuver, I switch on the radar and roll my eyes to get the blood circulating again. Focusing my vision on the scope, I'm greeted with a bright rectangular glob of light.

"Got 'em!" I shout as I activate the FLIR (Forward Looking Infrared Camera) and flip up the Master Arm switch.

"Master Arm's on. Pickle's hot."

"Roger that. Target in sight," Pat replies.

FLIR is the most accurate aiming system we have. It's how we aim the

Lt. Pat Day and his BN (Bombardier-Navigator) Pat Etienne, "Spanky," push towards the USS ENTERPRISE in a mock attack designed to sharpen everyone's skills.

laser, which we use to guide smart bombs. I slide the guidance reticle to about one boat length aft of the stern of the carrier, and feel the Intruder slightly nudge itself in that direction. Each aiming adjustment I make corresponds to a steering command on the pilot's display. Now to give the computer its "attack" command.

"Steering's good. Stepping into Attack," I announce, pressing a small red button on my slue stick. This tells the plane that a target has been designated—steering to a release point should be calculated and displayed on the pilot's screen.

"Good Attack," Pat says as again he slips the plane to the left. Still not a fighter in sight.

"Borg 1" pushes over on the final leg of the bomb run exercise against the USS ENTERPRISE.

With each adjustment to the aim point I make, Pat answers by moving the airplane in that direction. As we fly over the carrier's wake, a yellow "Complete" light flashes on the Armament Control Panel. Bombs away. Pat banks the Intruder to make room for Borg 2.

After scoring a "direct hit" against the ship's defenses, the winners execute a victory flyby to rub it in.

"GRAND SLAM, GRAND SLAM."

The exercise is over. The first glimpse we get of the fighters sent to find us is on the flight deck after we have already shut down.

"Gotcha."

—Lt. Pat Etienne, call sign "Spanky," A-6 Bombardier-Navigator,
ATKTRON 75, Sunday Punchers, northern Puerto Rico Ops area

Intruders Away

Last fall, when I overheard the story, I was sure I had walked in on the punch line of a bad aircraft carrier joke. An ex-Army Mohawk pilot, Mike Langer, is famous for his attempts to bolster the image of Army aviation at the waggish expense of all others.

"Did you hear the Navy just opened up a new Intruder base on the East coast?" he asked.

"Oh yeah?" I said stepping in blindly. "I thought the A-6 was going away."

"They're going away all right," Langer chirped. "Does the clue NAS Atlantis mean anything to you?"

Fortunately for me, someone stepped in and explained. An entire squadron of retired Intruders had recently been sunk off the coast of Florida in order to make some sort of fish sanctuary.

It was awkward to ask an Intruder pilot about the demise of his own plane, but he was happy for the attention and the conversation generated a phone number and a name. Langer's bad Navy joke was turning out to be real. The area code was 904—Florida.

"Grumman-St. Augustine-Steve Blalock," the man's voice said over the line. I introduced myself

A scrapped A-6 slowly sinks down to its final station at NAS Atlantis.

order from the Navy. Employees at the facility refer to that date as "Black Friday." It marked the beginning of the end for all Grumman Intruders.

"Come on down and see for yourself," offered Blalock, "we've got another batch going out soon." When I arrived at what has become Northrop/Grumman, I spoke with Blalock about the corporate and emotional devastation experienced in the wake of "Black Friday."

"Literally, we were working one day full tilt on the refit program, which promised Intruder feasibility beyond the year 2000, and the next thing we know, we were calling back jets that were in the middle of flight testing. I mean a 'stop work' order from the Navy means you STOP WORK...now. In the course of one day, the program had died and we were working the phase-out contract to do the teardowns on some eighty-plus airplanes."

Once word got out that the Intruder program had been canceled, several museums around the country made requests to obtain airplanes for display purposes. Six were released to various museums while a few were delivered to Naval air bases for gate guard duty. In the end, all written requests submitted by relevant organizations received aircraft. But when you're dealing with almost a hundred airplanes, there were more than could be reasonably given away.

Regardless of the disposition of the retired aircraft, each one had to undergo extensive demilitarization and decontamination. Blalock explained, "Grumman is subject to the same strict EPA regulations of hazardous waste disposal as everyone else in the country. To get these planes ferriable by truck for transport to wherever, all hydraulic fluids, fuel bags, and about fifty other items have to be satisfactorily neutralized, removed, reutilized, and inspected before they could leave our facility. Once they were clean and all the requests for airplanes had been filled, we began to sell the rest off for scrap. Quite honestly, it was depressing."

But in the midst of the doom and gloom at Grumman, Blalock hatched a plan that would help preserve the Intruder legend. In addition, he saw an opportunity to provide his home town with an environmental and economic boost.

The coastal waters off Florida's eastern shore consist primarily of barrier beaches with some naturally occurring coral and rock reefs close to shore. A featureless desert of sand on the ocean bottom stretches beyond these inner reef areas for some sixty miles out to the Gulf Stream and Continental shelf. Historically, this distant offshore oasis has supported the majority of the region's fish stocks, both sport and commercial.

In the early eighties, South Florida's first experimental artificial reefs were deposited three to five miles offshore in an attempt to attract marine ecosystems to these otherwise nonproductive areas. By monitoring

and explained the reason for my call. After a few minutes, Blalock had drawn a rough sketch of the big picture.

The facts: In the late 1980s, all Intruders were being rotated into Grumman-St. Augustine to be overhauled and refitted with new composite wings and center sections. This modification was designed to extend the life of the A-6 program well into the 21st century. On Friday, September 17, 1993, Grumman received a "stop work" the new reefs as well as the local commercial and sport fisheries, local marine scientists proved that placing clean, man-made objects on flat sandy areas of the ocean floor does in fact attract and support significant marine life.

The vast majority of Florida's one hundred-plus man-made reefs are created by depositing concrete rubble generated by the ongoing demolition and replacement of the state's aging waterway bridges. However, increased commercial demand for this recycled material has sent prices skyrocketing. As a result, communities interested in creating economical artificial reef systems in their backyard waters are being forced to search for cheaper alternatives to the bridge rubble. Blalock said, "For years, I've been a member of the St. Johns County Reef Research volunteer dive team, for whom we provide mapping and monitoring data on artificial reefs. It wasn't too big a leap to make the connection that Grumman's sanitized airplane fuselages could be used as material in our own reef program."

The St. Johns County Reef Research team applied for a grant from the Florida State Department of Environmental Protection, who was interested in a study proposed by the group. The team suggested an investigation into the validity of local fishermen's lore. Since they land so many fish while working the waters around sunken airplanes, regional anglers assert that indigenous red snapper actually prefer airplane aluminum habitats over the typical concrete rubble reefs. Due to the extensive military training that occurred in St. Augustine during World War II, numerous planes went down at the hands of inexperienced pilots, littering the local waters with aluminum "reefs."

A tugboat tows out a barge load of retired A-6s from St. Augustine, Florida.

While the state reviewed the grant application, Blalock worked on getting the planes with Jim Black from the Naval Air Department (NAVAIR). "We (the Navy) thought it was a great idea," recalls Black. "But there were formal channels to follow in order to get the proper permission to release the aircraft." In short order, both the state's Department of Environmental Protection and the Navy gave the project the green light.

Armed with a mission, materials, and the money to carry it out, the team was granted a site permit by the Army Corps of Engineers, who undoubtedly took great pleasure in the irony of the request. On June 16, 1995, nearly two years after Blalock had first floated the concept, the first barge load of twenty-six Navy and Marine Intruders was manhandled into the water twenty-five miles offshore using a bulldozer and a backhoe. Five days later, another eighteen Intruders followed.

"As a Grumman guy, it broke my heart," says Blalock. "But as a diver, I was excited. After all, we were creating something really important out of this otherwise sad loss. Besides, they were all headed for the furnace anyway, so at least we were saving them from that."

The following week, the team dove the site for the first time. Senior member Jim Netherton, a chemist at the University of Florida's Whitney Laboratory said, "The baitfish are the first to arrive, usually within fifteen minutes of sinking a reef. Next come amber jack and snappers after the first week. Within a year, everything from the tiny reef pickers that eat algae to the toothy pelagics like grouper and barracuda are living there full-time. On that first dive, we saw clouds of baitfish with the occasional jack and red snapper, but our primary objective was to map the site. As for the study, we'll do fish counts every six months and compare them with a concrete reef we put in about three miles north of here."

Almost one year to the day since that first drop, I traveled to Grumman to witness the final drops for myself. Another twenty-six planes had been rinsed of toxins and stripped of their former glory. They were laid out in two lines across the field by the old World War II seaplane ramp, waiting for the barge to come and load up.

These planes had been acquired by the Volusia County Port Authority at Ponce Inlet near Daytona Beach, where local charter captain Frank Timmons had heard about the success of the St. Augustine reef. His son operates commercial charters in the waters around the first Intruder drop and had already begun to proclaim the virtues of the new reef. Eager to replicate the positive results of the St. Augustine reef in his home fishery, Timmons advised the local Economic Advisory Board in charge of the reef program for Volusia County.

In response, Ponce Inlet Port Authority director Dan O'Brien made the initial inquiry about the remaining aircraft. Without any more grant money for a second reef, the St. Johns County team helped facilitate the donation of the material for the proposed Volusia County drop, which was now being dubbed "Intruder Alley." According to O'Brien, "We wanted to create a linear reef that stretched for almost three-quarters of a mile instead of just one big pile to see if that would attract more fish." Another difference from the original was the depth. O'Brien added, "There is a considerable insurance liability associated with these sites. We hope to deter the sport and spear gun divers with not only the thirty-mile boat ride, but also with the extreme depth of the water, which is around one hundred and thirty feet."

Around sunset the night before the planes were to be loaded, I slipped onto the airport grounds and walked among the dismantled fuselages. The outer wing panels were missing, as were the landing gear and engines. They looked more like the fish they were about to become than the seabirds they had once been. A sad wind was blowing the rudders back and forth and it seemed as if they were indeed trying to learn to swim.

The next morning I returned to the ramp to load the barge with the line mechanics from Grumman, who had conducted the teardowns. As a tribute to the A-6, these four guys had refitted their own golf cart with many of the

An Intruder pauses on the surface before sinking to the graveyard below. It will soon be home to countless marine animals.

parts that had come off of the stricken airframes, including ejection seats and a retractable tailhook. The thing looked like it could take a cat shot and fly away.

The loading of the barge went as planned and by late morning the first of three loads was headed down the intracoastal waterway. By the next afternoon, the barge was on site, thirty or so miles off Daytona Beach. I had hopped a ride with Captain Timmons, who was providing the supervising vessel used to guide the tug into position. Buoys marked the four corners of the permit site. The plan was to tow the barge diagonally across the square while pushing the planes over the side.

It seemed weird to me that there wasn't even a moment of silence before the crane began gouging the skin of the first A-6. I had tried to arrange a flyover of Intruders from VA-75, the first and soon-to-be last Navy squadron to fly the Intruder. But the schedule of the drops had changed so many times that the flyover fell apart at the last minute.

Standing on the lookout tower of Timmons's huge sport fishing boat, I recalled my own flight in an A-6 just a few months earlier. I remembered the brute force of the catapult and the sudden silence as we launched off the waist of the USS ENTERPRISE. As I looked up over the barge load of dead airplanes, I imagined the pilots from VA-75 in a flyby anyway. After that, I started to make pictures, to share this moment with the pilots at the last Intruder Ball, when the last squadrons will be disestablished later this year.

The sound of the crane tearing at the planes was enough to make you sick if the rocking boat hadn't already. Like some crazed animal, the crane's bucket would grab a jet by the scruff of the neck and try to force it into the water. The Intruders seemed to resist, repeatedly breaking loose and crashing down on the planes beneath them.

By the time the last few jets were left on the barge, I had gotten all the pictures I wanted from the surface. I wanted to shoot the final flight of the very last plane as it sank out of sight. I was in position when the A-6 hit the water. Longer than any of the others, it remained upright, floating on the surface. I swam near and it slowly banked towards me. Air rushed out everywhere in loud breaths of mist. With one last gasp, the lone Intruder slipped below the surface and started to sink. The plane flew directly under me in a gentle right turn, streaming a trail of bubbles. In half a minute, it had disappeared.

As for the remaining one hundred or so A-6s still in the fleet, most will be mothballed out at the Davis-Monthan boneyard as part of a peacetime reserve. There is some talk of the potential for foreign military sales, but that has traditionally been ruled out because of the lethality of the Intruder as well as the extreme cost associated with operating it. If any Intruders are sold, they will more than likely be tanker variants used in the aerial refueling role.

My mind flickered with the sepia images of postwar airfields around the country brimming with hundreds of B-17s and B-25s awaiting their turn at the furnace. As I shot my pictures, I couldn't help but wonder if these were to be the images that the next generation would associate with today's post-Cold War downsizing.

Greyhound

The Grumman C-2 Greyhound COD is the real workhorse of the fleet. Dedicated crews stationed ashore ferry people, parts, and everything else that must be brought out to the boat. The COD is not a pretty airplane, nor is it a fun ride, but working on this book, I logged more cats and traps in a C-2 than in any other Navy plane.

H*awkeye*

While I was in my first year at the U.S. Naval Academy, I hadn't done very well. My grades were just high enough to pass and my performance was not rated very highly by my upperclassmen. Since I was ranked toward the bottom of my class, I was depressed, and not sure if the military rigors of the Academy were for me.

I still remember clearly the day I decided I wanted to fly. My class had a brief on the different career paths in the Navy, and I remember thinking how incredible it would be to fly an airplane off an aircraft carrier. I went by myself to the library right after the brief and promised myself that if I didn't get to fly, it wouldn't be because I didn't work hard. Three years later, I had moved up about five hundred places in my class to graduate in the top half. It's not the kind of accomplishment you expect to be congratulated on, but I was proud of myself, and most importantly, because of the class rank I had achieved, I got my pilot billet!

When it came time for me to request a particular aircraft during Flight Training, the laws restricting women from flying tactical aircraft were still in effect, so I decided to try for the one aircraft that women were landing regularly on aircraft carriers, the C-2A Greyhound. I wanted to be a bona fide Tailhooker. To me that was the ultimate challenge in aviation. Period. The law was changed while I was still in the training pipeline, so when I went to the squadron where they train C-2 and E-2 pilots, I was able to select the E-2C Hawkeye.

Since then, I've been learning to fly the E-2, first in the FRS, and then in two fleet E-2 squadrons. When I checked into my first squadron, the senior pilot sat me down to explain the philosophy of training a "nugget" pilot. He told me that learning to fly the E-2 was like an apprenticeship: as you learn your trade, your elders give you more and more responsibility, until you are competent enough to handle things on your own and teach the younger pilots. Although I understood this concept intellectually, I still felt I should be able to fly the airplane much better than I did. Gradually, as I became more experienced, my confidence grew and I learned to relax a little, which improved my flying.

When I moved to my second squadron, I was still quite inexperienced, but better able to see the humor in how difficult a Hawkeye is to fly, especially in the landing configuration. Because it is a prop aircraft with a lot of rudder available, every time the power setting changes, the nose slices to the left or right, requiring rudder input. As you fly down the glide path, making power corrections, you are moving your feet back and forth constantly; we call it "riding the bicycle." Sometimes I feel like such a spaz that a big red nose and clown shoes would be a more appropriate outfit than a flight suit and boots. And sometimes the Landing Signal Officers (LSOs) who grade our landings agree with me.

Landing Grades were the hardest thing for me to get used to as a nugget onboard the ship. Each pilot has his grades posted on a large "display" on a wall of the ready room. Even though the display is supposed to be informational, it doubles as decoration. Instead of wallpaper, we have our personal triumphs and trials hanging on the wall to give the room a little color. Even our Naval Flight Officers (NFOs) get in on the fun. Their board represents every pass they were along for, and each line period one of them is designated the "Lucky Mole." Depending on your performance, you might find various articles hanging over your ready room chair that denote mistakes made during a landing. The first time you have one over your head, it's embarrassing, but then you see someone else have a bad day and the bolt (denoting a "bolter," failure to catch a wire) or the ace (denoting a low landing on the one wire) has been moved to someone else's chair, and you realize you aren't doing as badly as you thought.

As an E-2 pilot, I face the tough challenges of landing on the ship, but I have great respect for the NFOs who fly in the back. Not only do they have to put their complete trust in the pilots of the airplane, but when it comes to the tactical situation, they are expected to know everything that is going on. The Hawkeye is not just an air wing asset; we have our fingers in everyone's pie. It's not unusual for the CICO (Combat Information Control Officer) to listen to three, four, or more radios at the same time. He has to be cognizant of the surface picture as well as the air picture, and anything else that might be going on. He accomplishes all this in a cramped space with two other guys in an airplane that is moving constantly, either too hot or too cold, with almost no visual reference on what is going on outside.

Because of the mission and layout of the aircraft, it would be easy for the pilots and NFOs to ignore each other, but instead, the E-2 is an amazing example of crew coordination and mutual respect. When a mission is on, and the guys in the back end are working hard, we help them in any way we can. And when we are in the final approach phase of the flight, all five crew members are intensely focused on the safe return of the aircraft. When members of the other Naval Aviation communities fly with us, they invariably mention how professionally we fly the airplane, and how good the crew coordination is.

Lt. Quincy Hazlett brings her Grumman E-2 Hawkeye over the ramp of the USS ENTERPRISE. She flies with VAW-125 out of NAS Norfolk. Her husband is an F-14 RIO.

The way I look at it, to be a pilot in the Hawkeye community is a privilege and a responsibility. With five lives at stake, five families waiting for loved ones to come home safe and sound, I've learned that you don't take risks you don't have to take. I consider it a sacred trust when four other people are willing to fly with me at the controls, no matter what the weather, day or night. It's my job never to violate that trust.
—Lt. Quincy F. Hazlett, E-2C Pilot,
VAW-125, USS ENTERPRISE

An E-2C from the "world famous" Screwtops makes a final cat shot off the USS AMERICA after a six-month cruise helping to enforce the "No Fly" zone over Iraq.

S eahawk

Helicopters perform two of the most critical missions of the carrier air wing: search and rescue (SAR) and antisubmarine warfare (ASW). Both SAR and ASW variants of the UH-60 Seahawk are wonders of modern helicopter design.

The Sikorsky UH-60 is a great all-weather platform for standing the starboard defense station, call sign "Angel," the aerial standby for downed aircrews. Constant practice hones the skills required to pluck an injured pilot from heavy seas and high winds.

During work-ups aboard the USS CARL VINSON off the California coast, I awoke to a man-overboard alarm. It was just past midnight. After mustering with my commander, I went topside in time to see the crew for the Alert 15 helo rushing out to their bird. With the dark visors on their helmets down, the aircrew was being escorted by guys with flashlights. Within minutes, the rotors were spinning and the LSE had waved the helo up off the flight deck into an absolute black-hole sky.

The alarm had been sounded by the stern watch, who stands on the fantail, looking for signs of life in the water. On this night, he had seen a few of the green chemlights used by the night mechanics float by his position. While the helo conducted a pattern search around a flare shot into the ocean near the floating chemlights, the ship's company tallied a good muster, meaning all hands had been accounted for.

The next day I went by the ready room for HS-4, the helo squadron for the cruise. I learned that there are different levels of alert status that are maintained at all times. Alert 5

Sunset on the USS CARL VINSON as the helo crew from HS-4 chocks and chains the search and rescue (SAR) bird.

means the crew must be airborne in five minutes, Alert 15 in fifteen minutes, and so on. The crew on Alert 15 the previous night had gotten off the deck in just under the required time.

Night vision is the helo pilot's only friend on a moonless night over water. It takes the human eye more than twenty minutes to fully adjust to darkness, and pilots take this adjustment time seriously. An aircrew on overnight alert sleeps in full flight gear in a room that is either completely blacked out or lit with red lights only. All the passageways between the ready rooms and the flight deck are illuminated with red light from an hour before sunset until an hour after sunrise.

In addition to SAR missions, the ship's helicopter squadrons are trained in submarine hunting, their ASW role. Of the three main aircraft deployed against enemy subs, the P-3 Orion, the S-3 Viking, and the UH-60 Seahawk, it is the helicopter that is the most deadly. Subs may be detected by one of the fixed-wing high flyers, but it is the Seahawk that pinpoints the location and if necessary, drops a torpedo to kill the threat.

With active-dipping SONAR hung from a retractable cable, Hawks work in pairs to triangulate the contact. During work-ups, helo crews constantly practice these tactics against friendly subs in the battle group. As with all exercises, the activity sharpens the skills of everyone involved. The subs learn how to evade, just as the hunters learn how to flush and kill. While it's all in preparation for the real thing, the players still have some fun with the rivalry.

Steam rises from the waist catapult while a Seahawk from HS-4 shuts down and flushes its jet engines with fresh water to clean out the salt residue so harmful to Navy aircraft.

A Seahawk from HS-4 makes a "pony drop" of fifty pounds of mail to the USS CALIFORNIA on the way to Pearl Harbor.

Prowlers

A dawn patrol EA-6B Prowler launches from the waist cat of the USS CARL VINSON.

The Grumman EA-6B Prowler is an elongated variant of the Intruder which was designed as an electronic jamming platform back in the early 1970s. Besides the pilot, there are three EWOs, or electronic warfare officers, who operate the powerful electron emitters against a variety of RADAR threats as well as radio communications networks. Prowlers fly with both the Navy and Marine Corps in support of strike operations launched from either the carrier or land-based forces.

In recent years, the Air Force has integrated into the Prowler community because of the loss through retirement of their jammer, the EF-111 Raven. Several new Navy EA-6B squadrons "stood up" at NAS Whidbey Island to accommodate the Air Force's needs. These "expeditionary" squadrons, as they are called, are not designed to serve alongside carrier-based squadrons, rather, they are to be flexibly deployed to land-based operations around the globe.

Since these new squadrons became active, the Air Force has sent some of its own pilots and EWOs through the Navy training program in order to supply expertise and manpower to the units who will be supporting the Air Force missions abroad. This "joint" approach to common mission-readiness is the trend throughout all the military right now. Interchangeable tactics and training procedures are being developed service-wide; this program is a model for the future.

Warbirds over Pearl

Bill Klaers and Bob Lombard of the Yankee Air Museum in Rialto, California, had marked the golden anniversary of Jimmy Doolittle's raid on Tokyo by flying two B-25s off the deck of the USS RANGER in 1992. That experience was the impetus for the Yankee Air Museum's tribute to V-J Day in 1995. The idea: to fly twelve piston-powered warbirds from the deck of a nuclear carrier in the mouth of Pearl Harbor, kicking off a week-long celebration in Hawaii on the fiftieth anniversary of V-J Day. For a year and a half, Klaers and Lombard navigated through the minefields of Navy regulations, insurance determinations, and aircraft qualifications that threatened to sink their dream.

Just as the Navy became convinced that the civilian pilots were capable of pulling off such an event, corporate sponsorship began to crumble. In the final days of preparation, all outside financial sponsorship was withdrawn, stranding the airplane owners and the Navy at the pier.

"There was never any question in my mind," said Klaers. "At that point we were so close and the Navy had been so good to us, that each of us just did what we had to do to make it all happen. It would have been nice to have had the backing, but the bottom line is that we took the chance, we paid the price, and now we can say we did it."

While it was the pilots who flew the planes off the carrier, it was the Navy that made it possible. With the supervision of Capt. Bryan Rollins at AIRPAC, the Navy provided the carrier qualification standards and practice area at

Carl Scholl and Tony Ritzman pilot their B-25 named Pacific Princess *off the deck of the USS CARL VINSON.*

Contrails spiral off the prop of Ed Shipley's Corsair.

USS CARL VINSON and chained down to the hangar deck for the ten-day cruise to Hawaii.

Making the event even more memorable was the Navy's invitation to the civilian pilots and crew members to ride the carrier over to Hawaii. About fifteen men from the various teams got to experience flight operations as well as the daily routine aboard the world's premier combat aviation platform. Three of the distinguished guests had served on carriers during World War II, flying some of the very airplane types scheduled to be launched at Pearl Harbor. Ralph Knight, Tom Danaher, and Leroy Lakey had flown Corsairs, Hellcats, and TBMs to victory. For their first deployment since retiring more than forty years ago, the three friends were flying off in a completely original Grumman Goose. Danaher had recovered the amphibious flyer from Japan in the mid-fifties. The airplane had been given to the Japanese by the United States for use during reconstruction following the end of the war.

The night before the fly-off, pilots and crew members not already aboard were ferried out from the beach via several COD transport flights. The evening was spent moving the airplanes up onto the flight deck and briefing the emergency procedures for the morning's launch. By midnight most had drifted off to their staterooms for some rest, while a few groups sat around, quietly discussing the significance of the whole show.

NAS Alameda, just east of San Francisco. For an airplane to be considered, her crew needed to get the wheels off the ground using less than a thousand feet of simulated flight deck. Observers marked and measured the distances for each of the airplanes. After a long day of butterflies and white knuckles, twelve aircraft had met the challenge: two F4U Corsairs, two Grumman Gooses, a Grumman Wildcat, three North American B-25s, one SNJ advance trainer, one Grumman Albatross, and two Grumman TBM torpedo bombers. Later that week the planes were craned onto the

The Yankee Air Museum's B-25 In the Mood *is bathed in the Hawaiian sunrise on the morning of the big day.*

One month after the Hawaii launch, the event was repeated in San Francisco. Here the Confederate Air Force Bearcat warms up with Bill Klaers in the background running In the Mood.

Well before dawn on August 29, 1995, the flight deck was stirring with pilots.

The night sky was cloudy with stars and made clear silhouettes of the antique airframes. To stand among the propellers and pilots as the horizon slowly rose and fell with the waves was as close to heaven as anyone could come. Sunrise that morning on the flight deck of the USS CARL VINSON burned images on my mind that will never fade.

After all the planes had made precautionary run-ups and had been fueled, a short ceremony was held on deck to honor the effort that had gone into this remarkable gesture of historical pride. The flight line was cleared and the old rotary engines roared to life, spitting oil and smoke into the wind. The Wildcat went first, straight as an arrow, drawing cheers and hoorays as she lifted away from the flight deck and the huge crowd that had come to witness this once-in-a-lifetime sight.

Without hesitation the SNJ, Corsairs, and one TBM launched over the water. Each time a plane took off, the crowd erupted in cheers, as if they were witnessing

TBM pilot Ed Erickson taxis into the launch position with copilot Bob Monahan monitoring the gauges.

the sight of the first machine ever to fly. The three B-25s launched in succession, leaving only the Grumman Albatross to be launched. Suddenly, the aft, number four elevator rose up from the hangar deck, loaded with two F-18 strike fighters. The Air Boss came over the deck loudspeaker and ordered the launch of the two fighters as tactical cover for the carrier. In seconds, the Hornets were poised on the catapults for launch. With a noise that can only be compared to standing over a volcano during a hurricane, the fighters screamed off the deck. In full afterburner, they pulled into a vertical high-performance climb-out. The crowd went ballistic. Then the Albatross completed the launch cycle with a flawless takeoff.

Off the port side of the ship, the warbirds, flying now in clean echelon formation, made a beautiful low-altitude flyby before heading to Barbers Point NAS to roost. Finally, the two F-18s flew past, formed up tightly on one of the F4U Corsairs. Those visitors left on board the USS CARL VINSON milled around on the flight deck as the crew began to emerge, dressed in their gleaming whites. They began taking station along the perimeter of the deck, a Navy tradition for crews entering port. The ship slipped ever so slowly into Pearl Harbor, passing the Arizona Memorial. Upon the Captain's order, all hands turned and saluted. The events culminating in that moment moved many of us beyond words. Lest we forget.

Grumman TBM Avenger flown by Ed Erickson roars into the air after only a short takeoff run down the deck of the USS CARL VINSON.

Wally Fisk and Rick Boley borrowed their takeoff technique from the original Doolittle crews, who would place chewing gum on the Mitchell's tail skid. The best pilots were those who were able to remove the gum from the skid without scratching the paint. (Inset) Fisk's B-25, Buck You, *roars to life.*

Like a scene from the movie The Final Countdown, *Ed Shipley in his Corsair and CDR Barry Brocato in a Hornet from VFA-25 fly a formation spanning more than fifty years over Pacific storm clouds.*

Pulling through the props to clear the oil from the cylinders on the Grumman Wildcat prior to the launch.

A deck handler supervises engine run-ups for Wally Fisk and Rick Boley before releasing chocks and chains.

History flies over the North shore of Hawaii bathed in the last light of the day.

Tomcats

This Super Tomcat from VF-31 displays the extreme forces exerted on the landing gear, here compressed, almost allowing the ventral fins to contact the flight deck.

Salt water is a big enemy of the fleet. The planes are washed almost daily.

Coming Home

Exactly thirty years to the day it was first commissioned, the USS AMERICA (CV-66) returned from her final deployment to the Mediterranean. The cruise was punctuated by record after record in categories like number of sorties, consecutive days on station, and total arrested landings. But despite the high level of operational readiness, the AMERICA will never again take to the sea as part of any battle group. Instead, she is to decommission. The ship will be sealed and held in suspended animation as one of three reserve carriers on mothball detail.

I was lucky enough to make it aboard the AMERICA for the final days of her last six-month cruise. She was anchored off the coast of Bermuda as I hopped a ride with a CH-46 crew. During our approach, we circled the old carrier a few times and got a good look at her aging figure, accented by rust and showing the wear from

Sailors rush down the brow as crowds cheer pierside at Norfolk Naval Base, welcoming home the USS AMERICA from her final deployment.
(Right) Sailors in their dress blues "man the rail" as the AMERICA returns to her home port for the last time.

such a long cruise. The air wing had flown in support of NATO operations over Bosnia-Herzegovina and had been tasked with a tremendous volume of sorties.

Even as one of the last conventionally powered carriers in the fleet, the AMERICA maintained an outstanding operational record, influencing the course of world events since the war in Vietnam. More recently, she served with distinction in support of U.N. efforts in the beleaguered African nation of Somalia. After returning from Somalia, she became the first U.S. carrier ever to be loaded exclusively with rotor wing aircraft, as her role in Operation UPHOLD DEMOCRACY took the ship off the southern coast of Haiti. During this period, the USS AMERICA was actually under the tactical control of an embarked Army Major General. This innovative "adaptive force packaging" proved overwhelmingly successful and has since become a model in the continued military movement towards "joint" operational cooperation.

After getting underway aboard the AMERICA, we steamed toward the coast of the United States. Once within range, the final fly-off began just as the sun broke through what had been

Happy to be home. First-time fathers are the first allowed to leave the ship. (Right) LCDR Steven C. Lowry spots his family for the first time in six months.

a rainy sky. As squadron after squadron left, their own deck support personnel cheered and waved with the enthusiasm and emotion worthy of such an historic occasion. Never again would aircraft operate off the deck of this mighty ship. For the first time ever, I could actually hear human voices howling over the deafening hurricane of the flight deck. By late afternoon it was all over. Not a single Tomcat or Hornet was left aboard.

I had been shooting the very last F-14s from VF-102 Diamond Backs go off Cats 3 and 4. When the last bird had been launched, everyone on the deck went ballistic. Purple "grape" fuel guys, the red-shirted "ordies," and everyone else flooded the deck, high fivin' and gathering up their buddies for group snapshots. I wandered over to a big group of yellow Cat officers and their crews who were stripping off their boots. A big pile of steel toes were getting strung together on Cat 3. Navy tradition says that launch officers have their boots sent down the Cat upon completion of their last tour. Since the entire ship was coming out of service, the tradition required all shooters to strip down to their socks and to launch the Alert 5 footwear.

It was an event afforded all the seriousness and procedure of normal flight ops. The boots, or Mickey Mouse shoes as they are called, were loaded onto the shuttle, brought into tension, and ceremoniously blasted off the angle. As steam drifted back over the crowd that had gathered, I noticed a few people who had grasped the significance of the moment. It is not every day that history culminates in such brief, tangible events. Witnessing this end of an era for carrier aviation brought me a little closer to understanding words like Tradition, Duty, and Pride.

With the planes and most of the pilots gone, the mood on the ship made a swift shift into overdrive. Just one more day, and these five thousand-plus people would get to see their friends and families for the first time in over six months. It took a mad dash to get through the passageways, as enlisted and officers alike ran errands and carried boxes down to the hangar bays. Where airplanes had been tied down not five hours before, now piles of cargo boxes, footlockers, and tool crates grew towards the rafters. With not much left for me to do, I headed for my rack to sleep off the waiting.

In the morning, we were in plain sight of land. A steady convoy of H-46s, H-53s, and H-60s was ferrying pallets brought up on the elevators from the hangar deck back to the beach. For about five hours this went on, as the ship

A Tomcat from VF-102 makes its way to the bow for the final launch off the USS AMERICA. Notice all the people observing the last event from "vulture's row."

slowly made its way toward pierside in Norfolk and the waiting crowds. Painfully slow is a good description for how carriers move when returning to port. I had only been aboard for a few days and could not even imagine the levels of excitement for the crew. It is a phenomenon blind to the insulation of rank. Separation sickness affects everyone equally and as the ship's company manned the rails, the cure for this affliction came closer and closer, until finally we were tied alongside the pier.

The sea of people on the dock below waved hands and signs and roared in a storm of expectation. As the brows were raised in place by nearby cranes,

sailors yelled down and swung their arms in huge arcs, trying to catch the eyes of a sweetheart. It takes almost an hour to get the gangplanks set up. A long, teasing hour. Again, the old traditions of the Navy allow the new fathers whose babies were born during cruise to be the first to disembark. Media teams from local TV stations converged on these poor folks for their public reunions. The spectacle goes on for hours as one by one, everyone climbs down from this city away from home.

For some, it will be merely a few months before they are back on the moving deck of another ship. Some will transfer to shore duty, while others will leave the Navy altogether. Regardless of where they end up, each one takes with them the pride and memories of having served aboard the USS AMERICA on her farewell Med Cruise of August 28, 1995–February 14, 1996.

It is Naval tradition that upon completion of a deployment, the catapult launch officers strip off their boots and shoot them off the ship.

Observing the ritual, these waist cat "shooters" launch their flight deck boots down Cat 3 after the very last jet ever to be launched from the AMERICA has headed back to the beach.

Best of the Best

Some fifty years ago, when LCDR Butch Voris was first given the challenge to invent the Navy's premier flight demonstration team, few people realized the significance of his achievement. Today, the Blue Angels are without a doubt the most exciting and impressive air show spectacle on the display circuit worldwide.

Like the fleet aviators they represent, the Blues exhibit a mastery of their machines borne of hundreds of hours dedicated to the art of aerial combat. The formations and passes in the show are derived from maneuvers taught in the ACM syllabus of all Navy fighters. The entire squadron, from the scheduling officer to the mechanics and support crew, are part of one team, committed to perfection. While the Blues are the first to admit there is no such thing as the "perfect demo," they continuously strive to achieve that elusive end.

I was invited to go down and fly with the team at their home base in Pensacola, Florida. Every Tuesday the team is at home during the season, the public is free to come and watch their local practice flight, which is essentially a full-blown demo. On the Tuesday I arrived, we had marginal weather and were limited to a "flat show," which is designed to provide all the excitement and thrills of the regular demo, less the high-altitude vertical elements.

I arrived early for the 7:00 A.M. hop and was introduced around the ready room. Seated next to the #4 slot pilot, LCDR Scott Anderson, I listened in on the brief by Capt. Greg Wooldridge, call sign "Boss." He spoke in a soft, rhythmic voice intended to mirror the cadence and timing of the actual flight. Some of the team members

The Blues practice every aspect of the show every time they go out to fly, even the march.

would close their eyes and visualize their actions during Boss's recital. The mood was more like a seance than a psych-up for the high-energy mission. The concentration was palpable.

After the brief, I was brought out to #7, the two-seater Hornet that Scott Anderson would fly in the slot. With a safety chat from the plane captain and a few minutes spent strapping on the ejection seat, I was ready for the ride of my life. The clouds were moving in steadily, and I was beginning to panic that after all the hassle of making this happen, the plug would be pulled at the last second. Then I saw the team stepping out the hangar door and within a few seconds, they were lined up for the march down to the jets.

The engines started and the checklists complete, the Blue Angels taxied to the active runway. Clearance granted, the burners lit, we thundered towards ecstasy. Before the wheels were in the wells, Scott tucked under the Boss to form the Diamond. If there hadn't been a canopy between us, I could have reached out and touched the wing of #2, literally. It was unreal. The roar of the other jets around us was tremendous but not deafening. I could hear the Boss calling out the maneuvers over the ICS and hear the reciprocal check-ins from the rest of the team.

We were honking around that field like a flock of birds in a hurricane. My camera felt as heavy as a car battery under the g-load and it was everything I could do to keep it to my eye. Sweat

When at home in Pensacola during the show season, Tuesday morning practices are open to the public, while all other practice flights are made over a remote field west of town.

124

would fly down my face in straight lines as Scott held the Hornet in position behind #1. The sensations were fantastic. The noise, the speed, and the images I could see through my lens all combined into a feeling of such intense pleasure that I doubt I will ever achieve a buzz like that again.

All too quickly it was over and we were walking back to the hangar for the debrief. By 9:00 A.M. I was back at my hotel room sleeping off the effects of the Florida heat and the adrenaline. The dreams I had that afternoon couldn't even compare to the real thing. Fly Navy!

Future of the Fleet

The McDonnell Douglas F/A-18 Hornet has been around since the early 1980s. When it first entered service, it had notoriously short legs and the standing joke was that as soon as a Hornet pilot raised the gear, he started staring at the gas gauge. Over the years however, the airplane has evolved into a proven platform for such a wide variety of missions that today's carrier decks are covered mostly with Hornets. The next generation of Hornets that will enter service early in the next century are the Super Hornets: the F/A-18E and F.

Increased in size by nearly thirty percent, the Super Hornet is closer in proportion to a Tomcat than the old Hornet. With increased payload capacity and longer range, the single-seat E and two-seater F will come in a variety of configurations that will fill the gaps left by the recent retirement of the A-6 and eventually the F-14. There are even plans to develop a jamming variant of the F to replace Prowlers, which are rapidly approaching the end of their service lives.

The Super Hornet, while currently pushing the state of the art in strike/fighter technology, could be considered a temporary solution. There is a heated debate in Congress over the next generation of fighter aircraft. The JSF, or Joint Strike Fighter, is a concept development program. A Pentagon contest pitted the major manufacturers against one another to design a concept plane that could meet a demanding list of specifications. This plane of the future will be required to work for all branches of the military, including Air Force and Navy, as well as have a VTOL version to replace the Harrier for the U.S. Marines and Royal Navy. After the judging was complete, McDonnell Douglas, who came up with a revolutionary tailless design, was eliminated. Two months later, McDonnell Douglas was bought by Boeing. Many military aviation experts wonder where the sense is in cannibalizing our domestic aerospace industry, not to mention trying to make a single airplane perform all of the specialized missions necessary to ensure air superiority.

Most notably different on the Super Hornet from original Hornets are the jet intakes. This boxy, rectangular shape is much more stealthy and allows the passage of greater volumes of air required by the GE F414 turbofan engines.

The F/A-18E single-seat flies lead to the two-seater F model over the test area at Patuxent River. This photograph was made from the open ramp of the Strike Marine KC-130 tanker used to refuel the jets during flight testing.